Cut and Make
INDONESIAN MASKS

A. G. Smith and Josie Hazen

DOVER PUBLICATIONS, INC.

New York

Bibliographical Note

Cut and Make Indonesian Masks is a new work, first published by Dover Publications, Inc., in 1994.

International Standard Book Number: 0-486-28307-0

Manufactured in the United States of America
Dover Publications, Inc., 31 East 2nd Street, Mineola, N.Y. 11501

Cut Out

Wayang Topeng (1), *Java*   PLATE 1

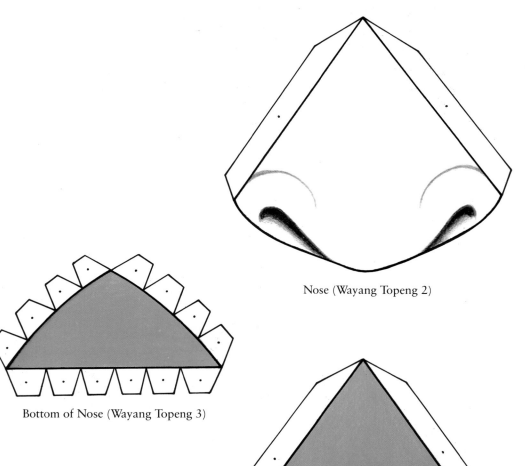

Nose (Wayang Topeng 2)

Bottom of Nose (Wayang Topeng 3)

Bottom of Nose (Wayang Topeng 1)

Nose (Wayang Topeng 3)

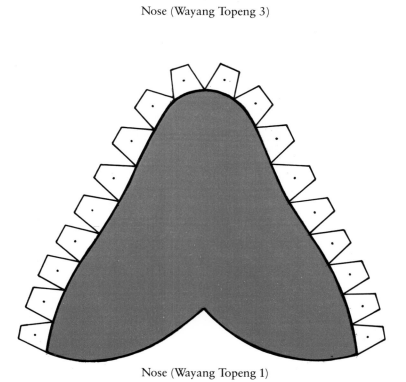

Nose (Wayang Topeng 1)

PLATE 2

Wayang Topeng (2), *Java*   (Ragil Kuning)   PLATE 3

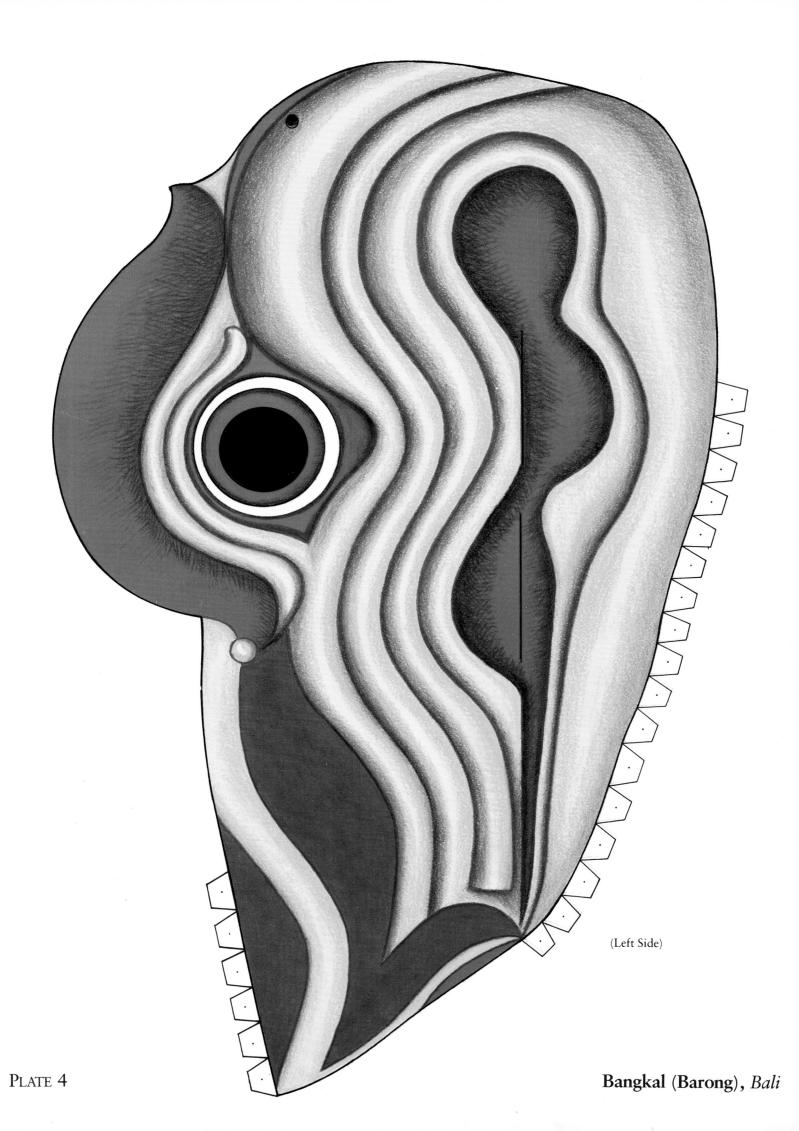

PLATE 4

(Left Side)

Bangkal (Barong), *Bali*

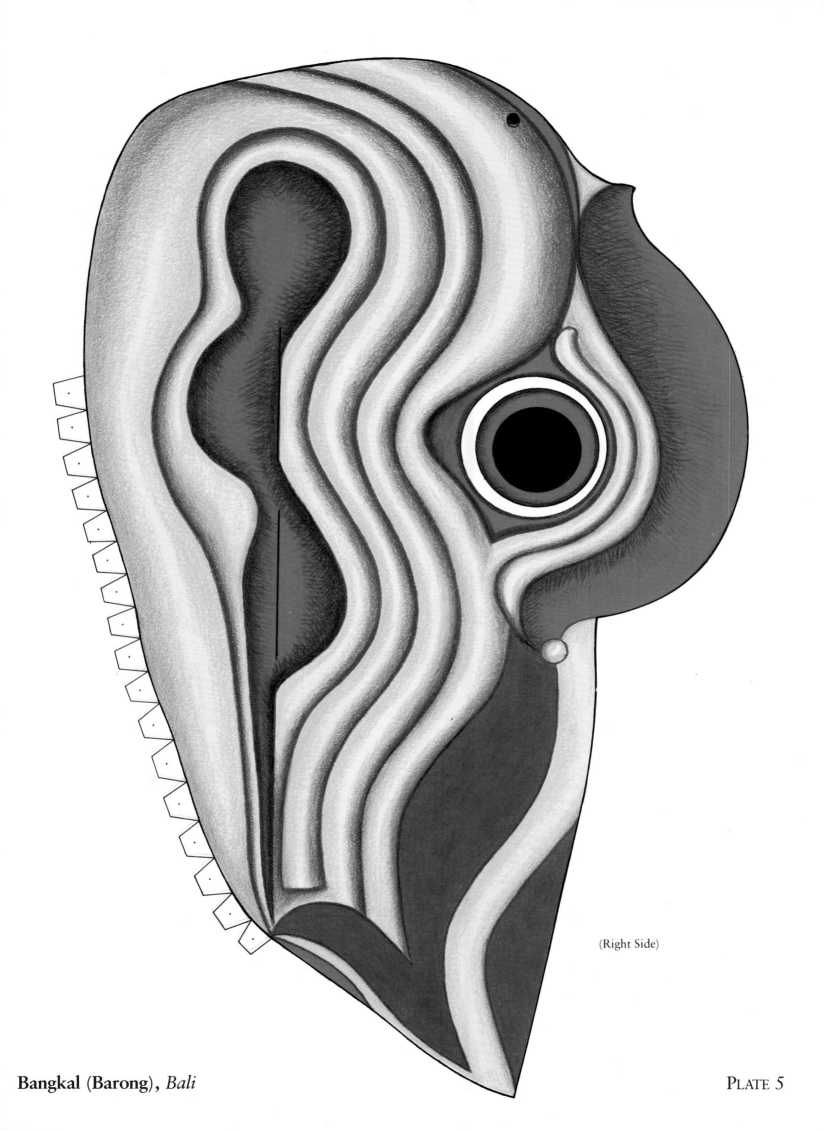

Bangkal (Barong), *Bali*

(Right Side)

PLATE 5

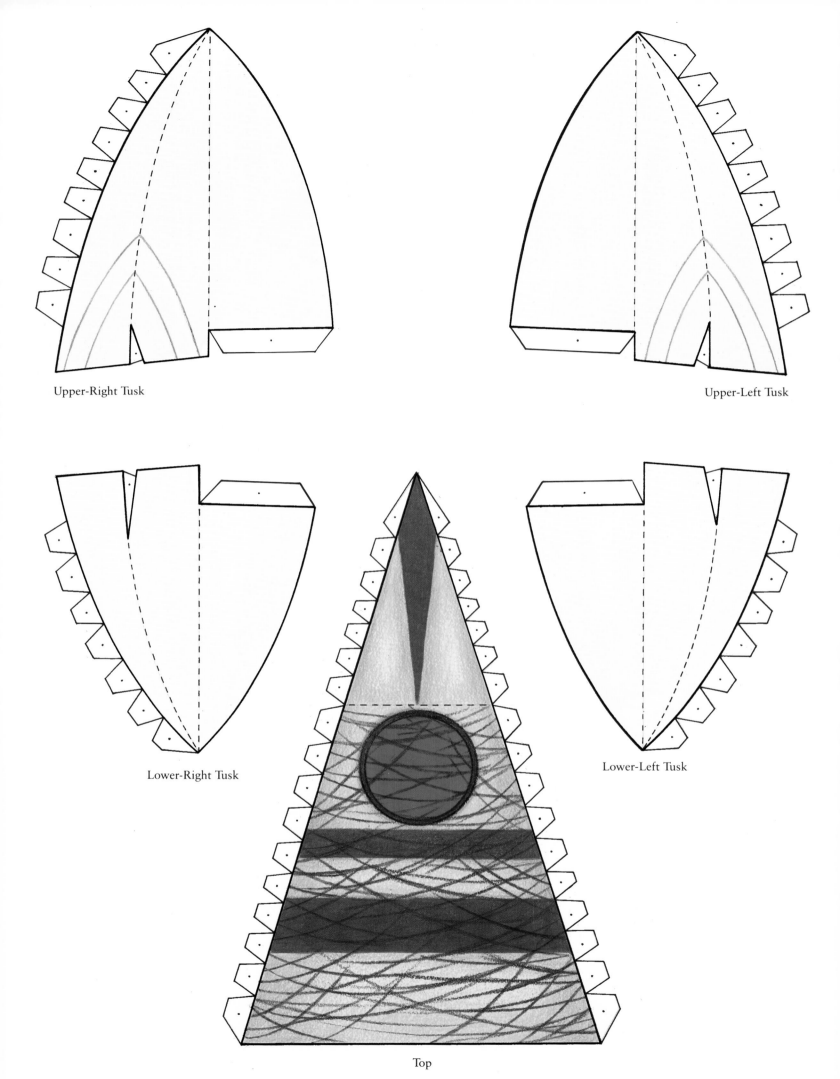

Upper-Right Tusk

Upper-Left Tusk

Lower-Right Tusk

Lower-Left Tusk

Top

PLATE 6   **Pieces for Bangkal**

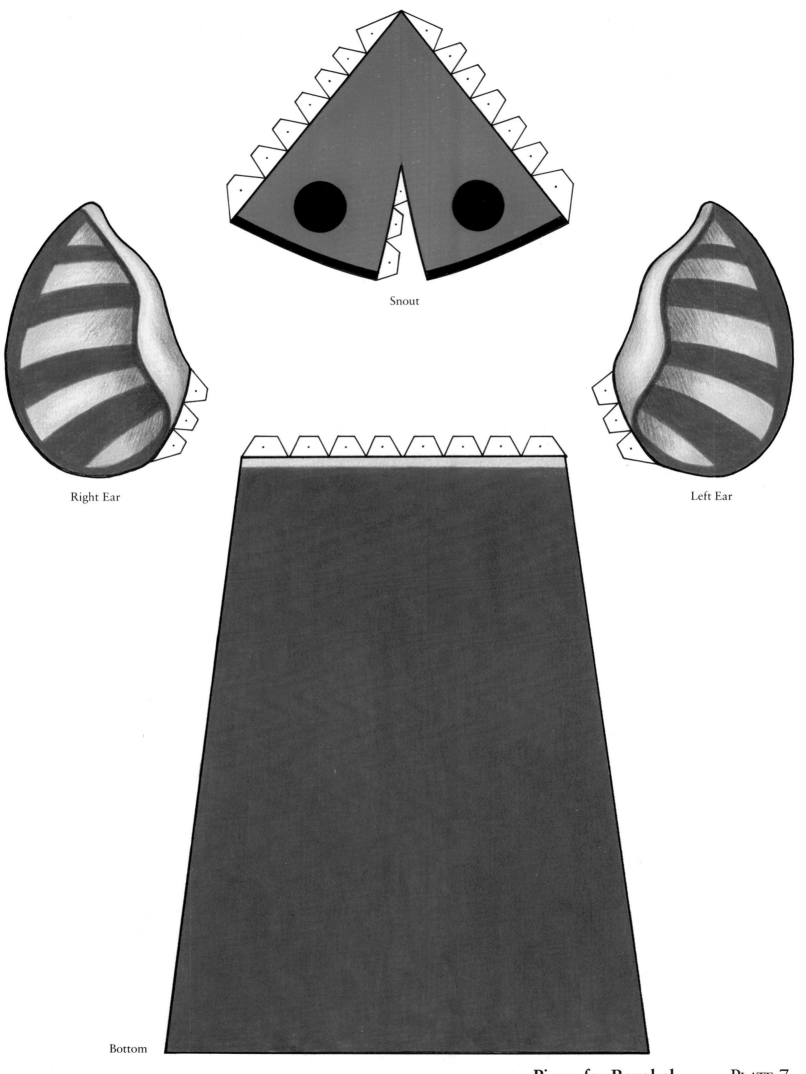

Snout

Right Ear

Left Ear

Bottom

Pieces for Bangkal PLATE 7

Cut Out

PLATE 8   **Rangda (Calonarang and Barong)**, *Bali*

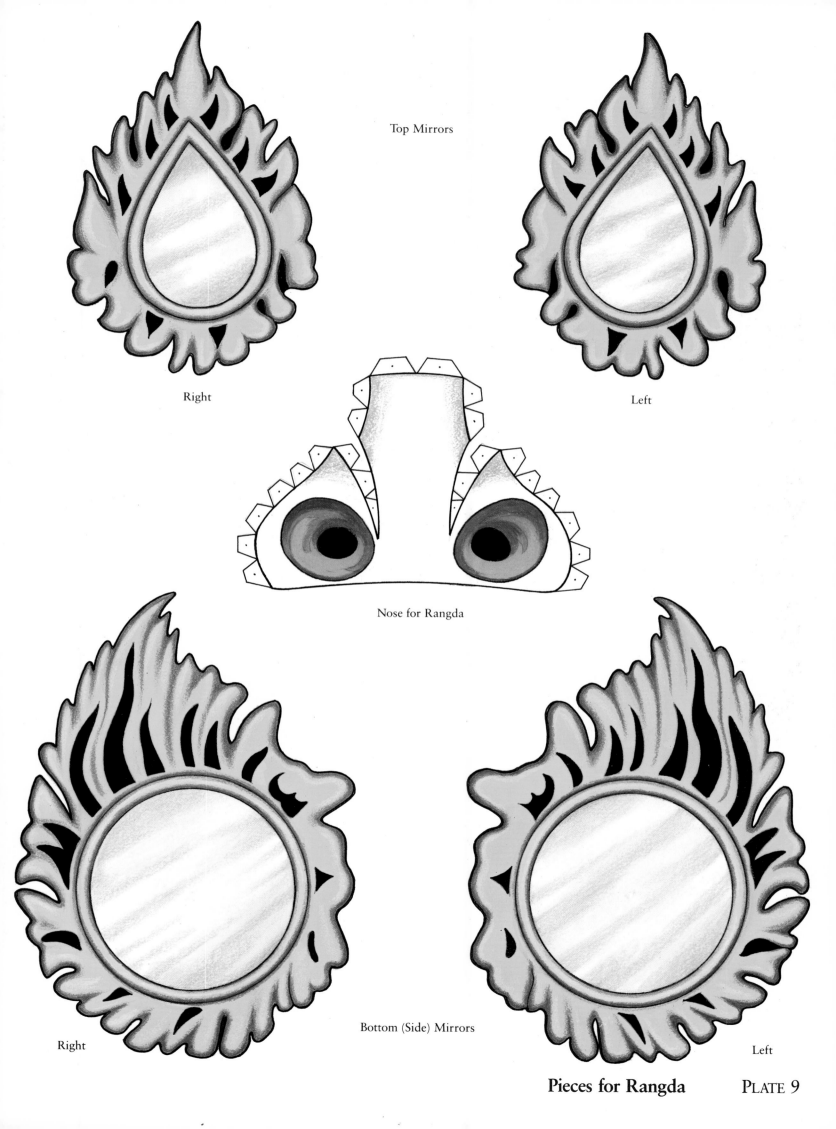

Top Mirrors

Right

Left

Nose for Rangda

Bottom (Side) Mirrors

Right

Left

Pieces for Rangda   PLATE 9

Top (Side) Mirrors

Right

Left

Bottom Mirror

<small>Plate 10</small> **Pieces for Rangda**

Cut Out

Bird Mask (Dayak),
Borneo

PLATE 11

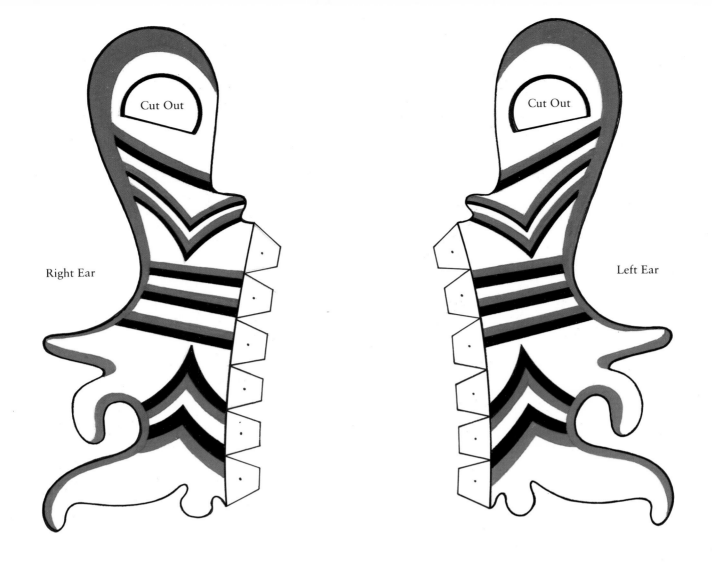

Cut Out

Cut Out

Right Ear

Left Ear

Beard

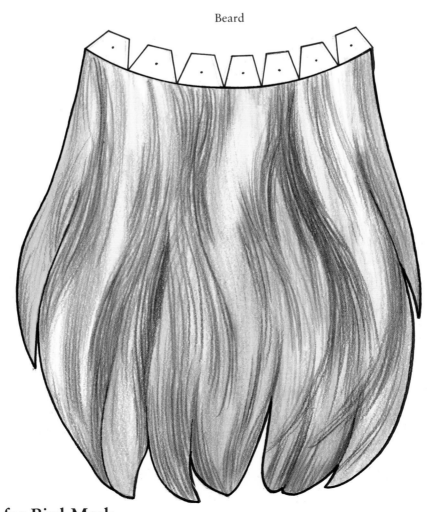

PLATE 12   **Pieces for Bird Mask**

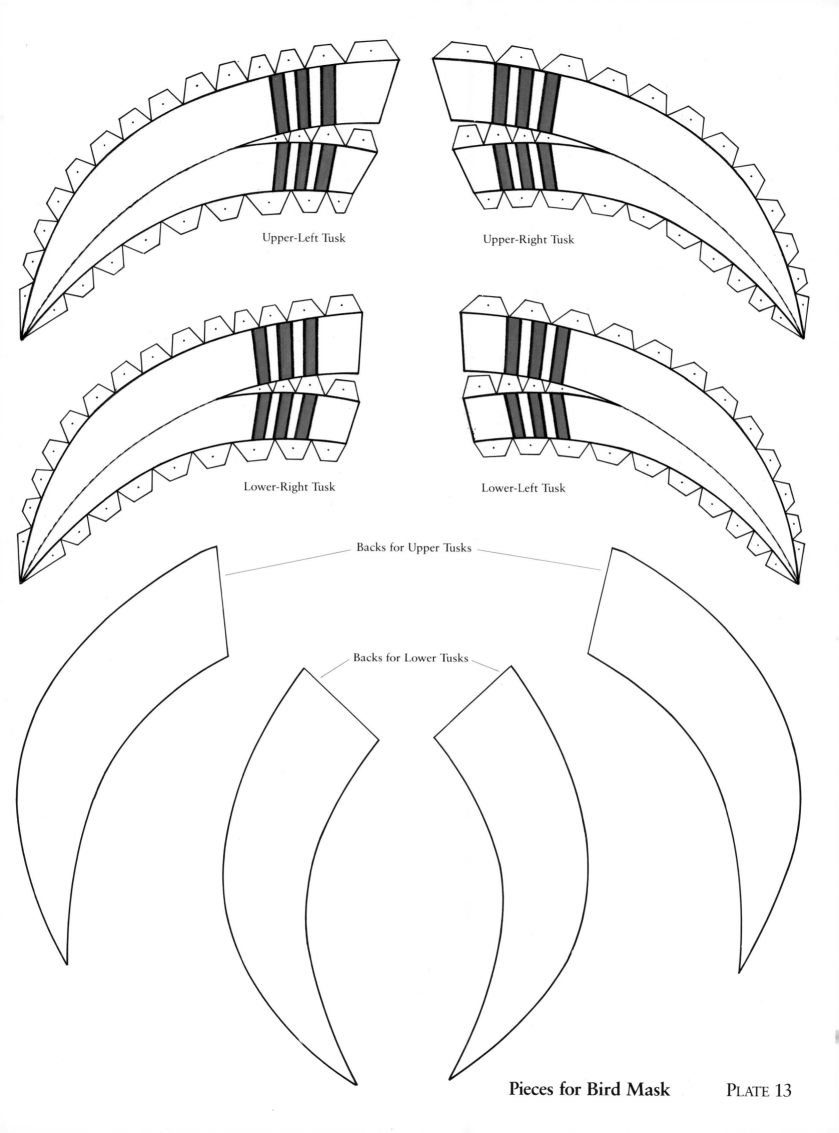

Upper-Left Tusk

Upper-Right Tusk

Lower-Right Tusk

Lower-Left Tusk

Backs for Upper Tusks

Backs for Lower Tusks

Pieces for Bird Mask　　PLATE 13

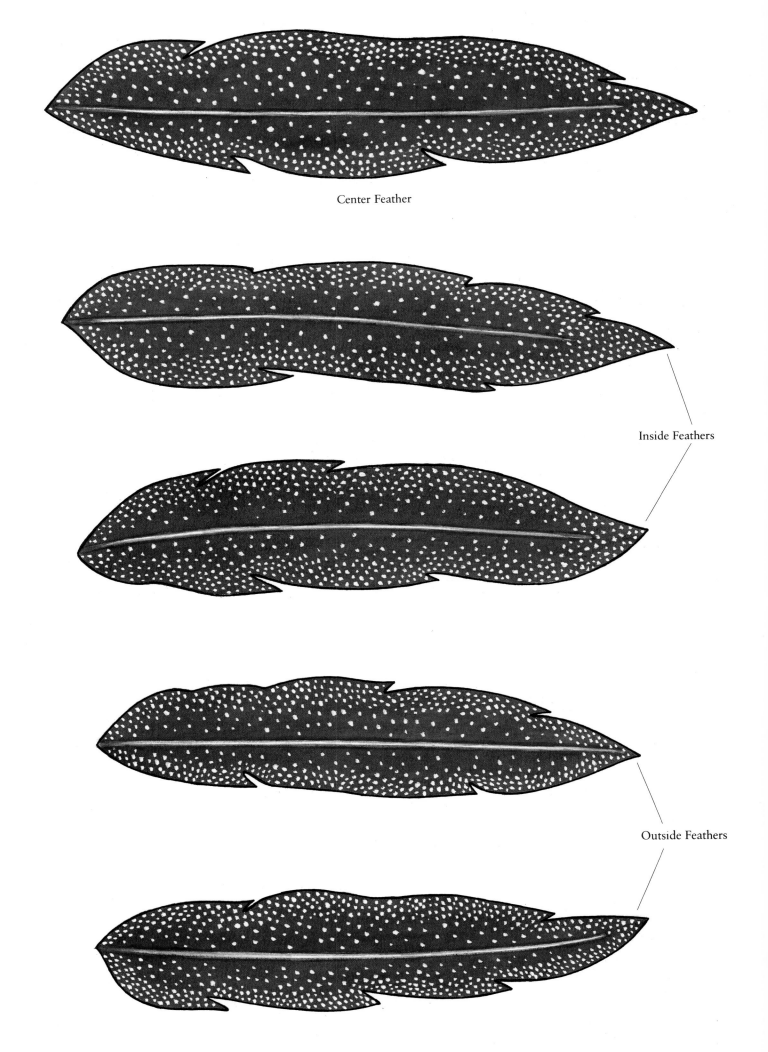

Center Feather

Inside Feathers

Outside Feathers

PLATE 14   **Pieces for Bird Mask**

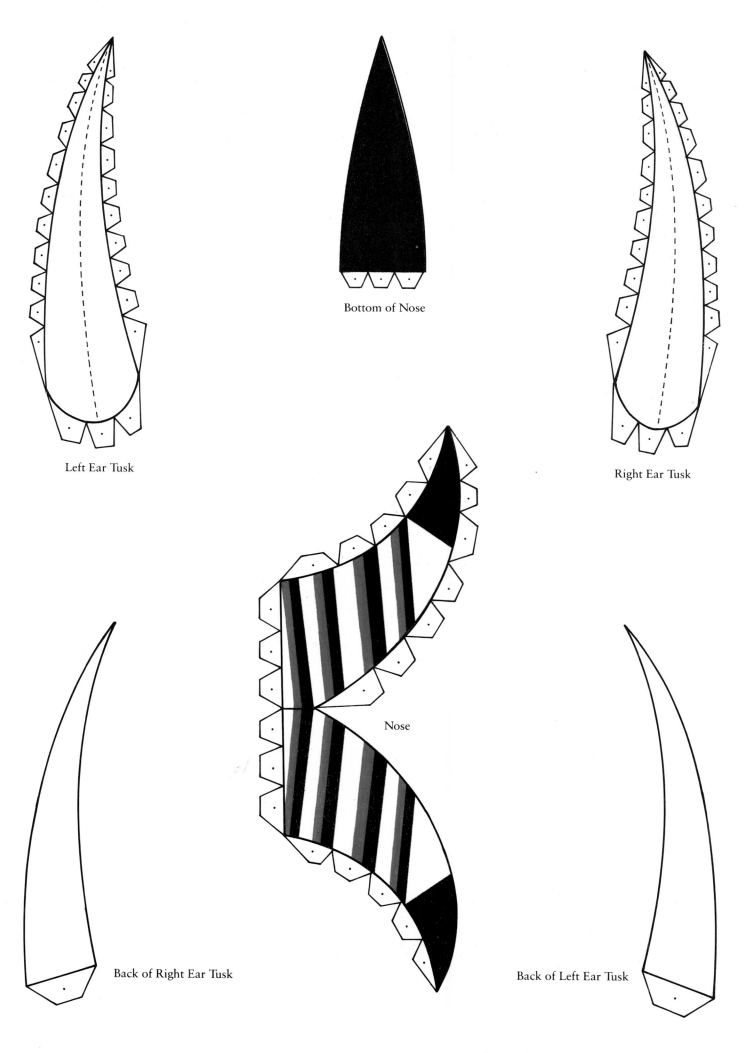

Left Ear Tusk

Bottom of Nose

Right Ear Tusk

Nose

Back of Right Ear Tusk

Back of Left Ear Tusk

Pieces for Bird Mask   PLATE 15

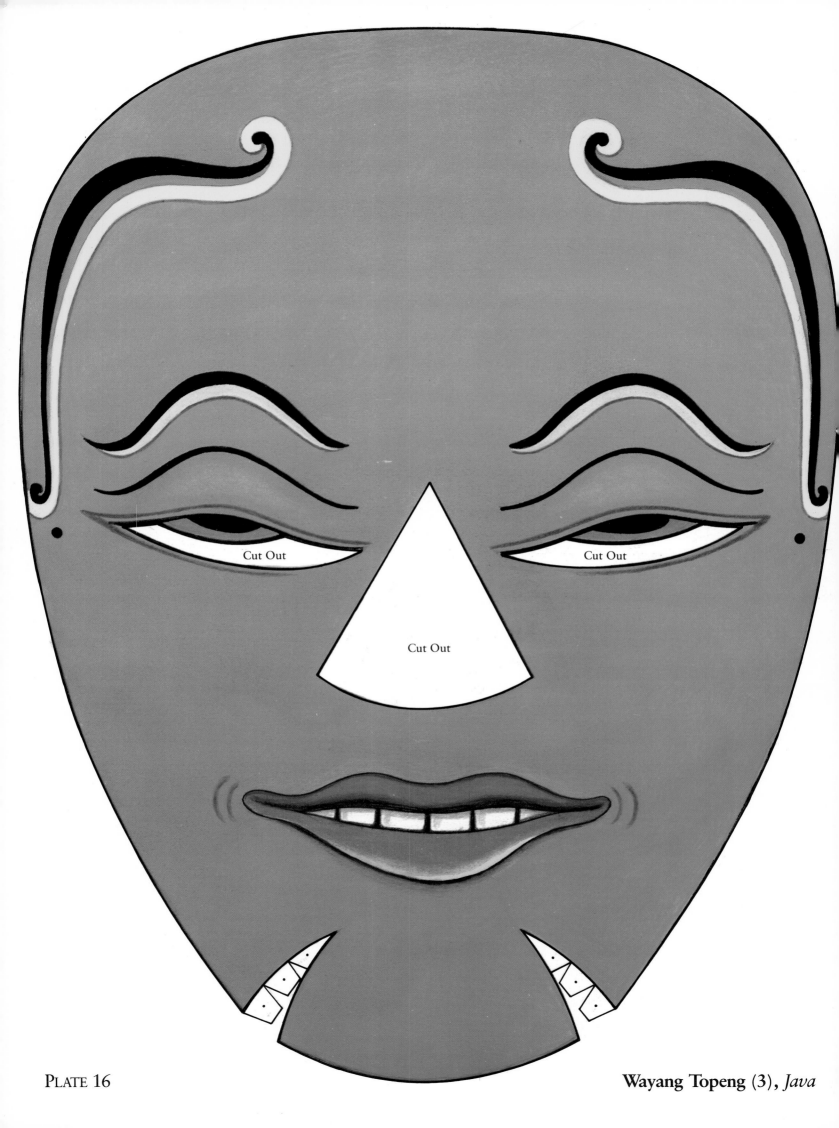

Cut Out

Cut Out

Cut Out

PLATE 16

Wayang Topeng (3), *Java*

INDONESIA, A COLLECTION of islands, is also a collection of cultures, each with its own traditions and its own arts. Many of these cultures have performing arts with features in common—this includes the use of *masks*. The six masks that you can make from the pieces in this book represent three different Indonesian cultures from three different regions: Java (the main, and most populous, island), Bali and Borneo.

The masks of Java are from a culture—itself really a group of related cultures—that, although dating back thousands of years, is more closely tied to the modern world than the other cultures represented in this book. Centrally important in Javanese art is the *Wayang*, or shadow play. Wayang is very old and incorporates Chinese storytelling, Hindu myth and elements deriving from the Muslim influence that has dominated Indonesia for the past several hundred years. Each region also adds its own traditional stories to local performances of Wayang. (The second Wayang Topeng mask represents Ragil Kuning, sister of Prince Pandji, the legendary hero of many East Javan Wayang performances.)

Wayang is very complicated and is staged in many different forms, but there is always some kind of accompaniment by *gamelan*—Indonesian music. A Wayang performance of whatever kind is usually done by professionals who have spent years perfecting their skills. The earliest form of Wayang, still seen today, was performed by casting on the wall the shadows of flat leather puppets. In another type, regular puppets are used, and there is yet another major type (Wayang Topeng) that is *danced* by a troupe of live actors. A Wayang performance, typically lasting for many hours, is part entertainment, part art and part religion. Musicians and troupes of actors—or a *delang* (the puppet master)—are often hired by prominent members of a community for special social occasions.

There are two Balinese masks here. Although some kinds of Balinese drama is closely related to certain types of that of Java, other kinds are more particularly Balinese, being connected more closely than the Javanese drama to traditions of Hinduism (the dominant religious influence in Bali, as Islam is in Java and in much of the rest of Indonesia) and even older religious rituals. The "Calonarang" is based on a Hindu story, while the "Barong," rather than being a single drama, is a loosely related group of rituals, each associated with a spirit represented by a mask. Rangda, represented here by a mask, is a major character in both Calonarang and Barong. Rangda is an incarnation of evil, a crazed, angry, malicious widow who embodies the spirit of Dewi Durga, the Queen of Witches.

Bangkal, or the Boar, is the other Balinese mask in this book. Used in holiday rituals, Bangkal, a Barong mask, represents a spirit that protects a village.

Many of the tribes of Kalimantan, the Indonesian part of Borneo, are known collectively as the Dayak. Traditionally they would wear masks like the Bird Mask in this book to ward off evil spirits and infuse themselves with strength on their head-hunting expeditions. Alas, the art of fashioning these complex masks has died out among the Dayak. (Fortunately, so has their practice of head-hunting!)

The individual masks are identified on the plates with the pieces. General directions for constructing all the masks, and then special instructions for each one, follow.

GENERAL DIRECTIONS

Tools and visual aids. The tools you will need are (1) scissors; (2) an X-ACTO knife; (3) white glue, such as Elmer's or Sobo; (4) a tool for scoring, such as a dull paring knife or an X-ACTO knife with an old, dull blade; (5) a ruler or other firm straight-edged object to be used as a guide for scoring; and (6) a burnishing tool (the back of a spoon will do) that you can use to press the pieces firmly together when they have been glued; (7) a tissue or damp sponge for wiping away excess glue; and (8) some string. Your work surface should be protected by a thick layer of cardboard or newspaper.

On the book's covers you will find color photographs of all the masks. Before assembling each mask, examine its photograph carefully to see how the pieces fit together. Line diagrams that display the specific features of each mask accompany the special directions that follow these general directions.

Cutting out the pieces. Cut along the black lines. Use the scissors for rough cutting, the X-ACTO knife for the finer details and for cutting out the eye holes. You may need to punch out the tiny holes for the string (to hold the mask on your face) with a pointed object; these are usually too small to cut.

Fitting and gluing pieces together. The glue tabs on each mask are white and marked with a black dot. As soon as you have cut out a piece that has tabs, examine the diagrams to see how the piece will be glued to the adjoining pieces. If the tabs are to be folded, *score* along the black border lines between the tabs and colored areas—that is, trace along the lines with a sharp or pointed tool, pressing hard enough to make a groove in the paper but not hard enough to cut through it. Your scoring will be straighter if you use a ruler.

Before applying glue to the tabs, make sure that you have cut out the eye holes, unless you intend to use the masks only for hanging as decorations, as well as the holes meant for inserting string for tying the mask around your head. Put glue only on the tabs marked with a dot, never on the surface that will receive the tabs. Do not use too much glue, or it will seep out and cause a mess. A damp sponge or tissue will help clean up any excess in case glue does seep out.

Use a spoon or other burnishing tool to press down areas that have just been glued. Allow glued sections to dry thoroughly before handling them. When a main piece needs to have more than one attachment glued to it, glue them one at a time, letting each one dry thoroughly before gluing on the next.

All of the masks have "gores," small triangular tabs that are glued under the adjoining area to give the mask a three-dimensional shape (see figure below). Glue the gores in place before attaching anything else. You may have to hold the gores in place with your fingers until the glue has set.

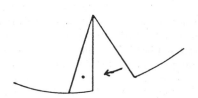

Attaching string for hanging and wearing. The two string holes for each mask are indicated by large dots (black or white) on the left and right sides of each mask. Carefully punch a hole in each dot with a pointed tool. Then push the two ends of a long piece of string through the holes from the back of the mask so that they hang down in front. (Use a piece of string at least two feet long; you can always cut off any excess later.) Knot one end of the string in front.

If you want to hang the mask on the wall, leave only an inch or two of slack in the string behind the mask. If you want to wear the mask, hold it on your face and pull the unknotted end of the string forward until it is taut. Knot the other end in front and cut off any excess string. If you wish to wear the mask some of the time and hang it up when not wearing it, you can shorten the string without cutting it by doubling the excess into a loop and taping it.

INSTRUCTIONS FOR ASSEMBLING INDIVIDUAL MASKS

Wayang Topeng (1) (Plates 1 and 2).

The first Wayang Topeng mask requires only the nose to make it complete. Cut out the hole in the face as marked. The nose is formed of two pieces on Plate 2. To assemble the nose, glue the tabs on the concave sides (that is, the two sides that curve *inward*) of the nose-bottom piece to the nose piece at the edges *without* tabs. You may have to hold the pieces together until the glue has dried. Then, from the front of the mask, insert the nose piece through the nose hole and glue the tabs to the back of the mask.

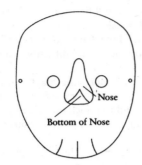

WAYANG TOPENG (1)

Wayang Topeng (2) (Plates 2 and 3).

This second Wayang Topeng mask is very simple to make. The nose consists of just one piece with two large tabs. Cut the hole in the face and glue in the nose, again with the tabs glued to the back of the mask.

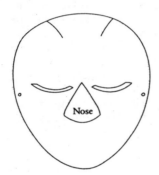

WAYANG TOPENG (2)

Bangkal (Plates 4 through 7).

The Bangkal mask requires a bit more effort than most of the other masks. Begin by gluing the two sides together along the five tabs over the snout (found only on the piece for the left side of the head). The top piece, on Plate 6, should be scored and folded forward on the line. It will help to give the larger portion curvature by pulling it over the edge of a table, printed side up. The tabs should then roughly line up with the top edges of the sides of the snout and head. Glue these tabs in place. Next, glue the snout and the bottom piece in place. (The snout first must be formed by gluing the gores in place.) Each of the four tusks is formed of a single piece. Score and fold along the fold lines and glue the gores in place. This will give each tusk "body." The straight lines along the side of the mouth are guides for lining up the bases of the tusks. Glue the tusks on as shown in the diagram. Finally, glue the ears in place.

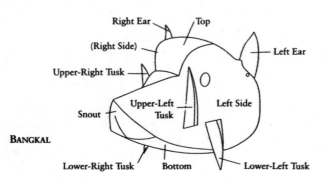

BANGKAL

Rangda (Plates 8 through 10).

Rangda looks more complicated than it really is. The nose piece is formed by gluing the rows of tabs that face *toward* the inner edges of the piece, under those edges. The bottom mirror is glued to the tusks that protrude from the mouth. The other six mirrors are glued where shown in the diagram.

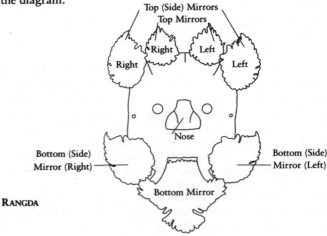

RANGDA

Bird Mask (Plates 11 through 15).

Although the Bird Mask is the most complicated, it is really very easy to construct once you have done the other masks (for that reason it may be a good idea to save this one for last). The nose is formed of two pieces (like some of the others) and is glued in place much as the others are. There are six tusks, each formed of two pieces. The ear tusks are inserted through the holes in the ear pieces in a manner similar to that in which you glued in the nose. The only slightly tricky part left involves distinguishing among the four remaining tusks. Keep in mind that the "upper" tusks actually point downward and the "lower" tusks are the ones that point upward! Gluing the feathers and the beard in place is very easy: just follow the diagram and the photograph.

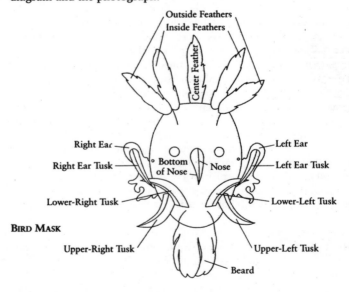

BIRD MASK

Wayang Topeng (Plates 2 and 16).

This mask is very similar in construction to the other Wayang Topeng masks. The main part of the nose has only two tabs, but there is also a bottom piece that is glued on much as that of the first Wayang Topeng mask.

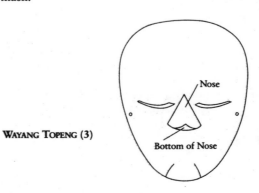

WAYANG TOPENG (3)